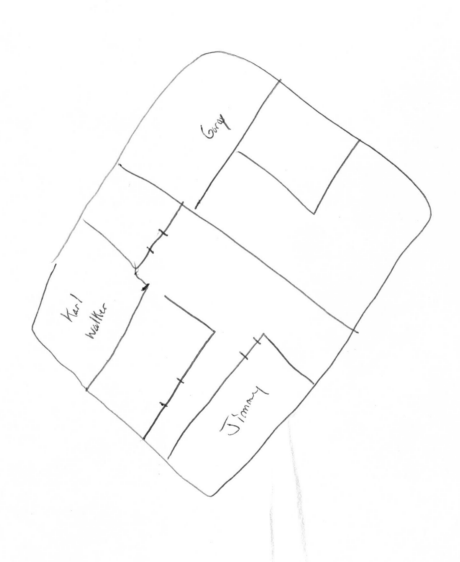

THE ART IN CARTOONING

THE ART IN CARTOONING

Seventy-five Years
of American Magazine Cartoons

Edited by

EDWIN FISHER, MORT GERBERG and RON WOLIN for

The Cartoonists Guild

CHARLES SCRIBNER'S SONS / *NEW YORK*

1 3 5 7 9 11 13 15 17 19   MD/C   20 18 16 14 12 10 8 6 4 2

PRINTED IN THE UNITED STATES OF AMERICA
Library of Congress Catalog Card Number 75–6035
ISBN 0–684–14329–1

CONTENTS

COLOR PLATES BETWEEN PAGES 96 & 97

ACKNOWLEDGMENTS

THE editors, Cartoonists Guild, and Charles Scribner's Sons wish to express their deepest thanks to all the artists and heirs whose kind cooperation has helped to create *The Art in Cartooning*.

The project was first suggested by the late Erwin Swann more than three years ago in the form of an exhibition on the same theme, presented at Xerox Exhibit Hall, Rochester, New York. His intelligent counsel and interest in comic art helped to guide us through the difficult planning period and his generosity in making the resources of the Swann Collection of Caricature and Cartoon available was an invaluable asset, especially in the selection of drawings from the early years. We are also grateful for the time, effort and consideration given by Alison Dodd, curator of the Swann Collection.

Many galleries, university libraries, and publications were extremely helpful in researching and locating drawings for inclusion in the book. Lack of space prevents us from offering more than our warm appreciation to: Barbara Nicholls of the Nicholls Gallery in New York City; Georgia Riley of the Graham Gallery in New York City; James Geraghty, Milton Greenstein and Ruth Rogin of *The New Yorker*; Stephanie Brody of *Esquire* Magazine; The Thurber Collection of The Ohio State University Libraries; The George Arents Research Library at Syracuse University; the Syracuse University Art Collection; and the Western History Collection of the University of Oklahoma.

We are indebted to the following copyright owners for permission to reprint cartoons owned by them:

Cartoon copyright © 1968 by Sergio Aragones and E. C. Publications, Inc. Reprinted with permission.

Cartoon by Peter Arno. Copr. © 1944 Pat Arno Maxwell and Andrea and Kitty Bush. Reprinted with permission from "Man In The Shower" (Simon & Schuster).

Cartoon reprinted from *Audubon* Magazine, copyright © 1972.

Cartoon copyright © 1967 by *Changing Times, The Kiplinger Magazine*.

Cartoon copyright © 1932, renewed 1960, by The Conde Nast Publications Inc.

Cartoon copyright © 1973 by the Hearst Corp. Reprinted by permission of *Cosmopolitan* Magazine.

Cartoon copyright © 1974 by *The Critic*.

Cartoons copyright © Abner Dean 1945 and 1973, from "It's A Long Way to Heaven." Cartoons copyright © Abner Dean 1947 and 1975, from "What Am I Doing Here?" Reprinted with permission.

Cartoons copyright © 1933, 1934, 1935, 1940, 1959, 1960, 1962 and 1964 by Esquire, Inc. Reproduced by permission of *Esquire* Magazine. Cartoon by Gilbert Bundy. First published in *Esquire* Magazine.

Cartoons copyright © 1968 and 1969 by *Evergreen Review*. Reprinted with permission.

Cartoon printed with permission of Mrs. Rube Goldberg.

Cartoons from *Judge* and "Old" *Life* reproduced by permission of H. T. Rockwell.

Cartoon copyright © 1975 by King Features.

FOREWORD

IF you study a Holbein portrait, it will reveal an almost spendthrift abundance of aims. It is at once an abstract composition, a powerful drawing, painting, character study; a virtuoso display of brushwork, texture, modeling, calligraphy and color. It is a representation, too, of persons and objects, interesting in themselves. It is overlaid, moreover, with a weight of thought, accent, symbol, sense of choice and even of opinion, so that the artist seems in lively conversation with the viewer.

A masterpiece of that sort conquers on a dozen grounds. But where today can such full-bodied art be found?

For one place, in cartooning. And this is not surprising. For, like Holbein, the cartoonist has a multitude of things to say and much to do in order to achieve his aims.

He must, of course, be capable of drawing with expressiveness and verve. That is self-evident, but it merely begins the list. He must present *people*—a cast of characters whose type we recognize in life. Often, he goes beyond type to create persuasive individuals, as in the Dorothy McKay drawing on page 67. Without this recognition we, the audience, are unengaged. All good cartoons relate somehow to the particularities of mankind. The cartoonist knows this. Even when he draws animals they are, at bottom, human beings.

The cartoonist's people also must have mood and passion, must be identifiable by class, ideology and generation. This in itself demands a skill at *genre* drawing of no mean degree. Then he must pose his people, clothe them, make their feelings apparent, place them in appropriate surroundings—and all this merely to set the stage for some particular gesture or action, which he must convey with absolute preciseness.

Action in cartoons *is* gesture, almost always. Cartoon gestures usually are emphatic; however, there are as many "acting styles" used in cartoons as in the theatre, from broad burlesque to subtle comedy of manners. The nature of the comedy dictates the style in which it is played. If a cartoonist has a wide range of ideas he must command a wide variety of acting styles, and many do. Once he has chosen the style suitable to a particular idea the artist, like the dramatist, must build his scene and keep its parts consistent. He stages his characters in a tableau, presenting the one crucial moment in time which implies all action that has gone before and the action that will follow. It is the frozen action of the single cinematic frame. It is the moment when, for instance, in *Plate 9*, the aggrieved Lautrec looks up at La Goulue to say, reproachfully, "Thank you madam, but the pencils are not for sale."

Even a story told within the confines of a single scenic box must be presented in dramatic sequence—first this, *then* that—if it is to have effect, particularly if it is to be humorous. Every story teller knows the importance of describing things in order. The cartoonist does especially. He must direct the eye. To do this, all the elements and tricks of composition and of tonal emphasis must be known to him. Quite often he must use them to the full.

For example, in one of Peter Arno's most famous cartoons*, it is all-important that the viewer must first see the airplane crashing in the background *before* seeing the little man in front who says, "Well, back to the old drawing board." We do, indeed, "read" the drawing in this necessary sequence, but it is due to genius, not to chance. To push the viewer's eye along that particular path, Arno has brought into play a powerful crossfire of diagonal lines and wedge-pointed spaces centered on the crashing airplane. The thrust of running figures, the lines of ambulance and hangar, even the tiny parachute strings in the distance, do their part. It is a composition of Bruegelian completeness. Indeed, it much resembles the tremendous star-shape of diagonals imploding on the bagpipe player in Bruegel's *The Peasant Dance*.

Alternately, composition may be used for just the opposite purpose: to fool or misdirect the eye so that attention is deliberately led *away* from an important object. Two excellent examples of this sort of deftness can be found on pages 58 and 39. In the first, I. Klein takes care to direct our attention to the unimportant right-of-center of his drawing so that the absurd situation of the taxidermist will not be seen too soon. In the second instance, Forbell uses a bland tone to keep us from discovering the multiplicity of activities of cuckoo clock tuners all at once.

Cartoonists also must be able to create dramatic moods or "atmosphere." Ghost stories, gallows humor and mock-historical analogies attain their full effect only in a convincing stage-setting. Comic action often must be played against a background of heroic grandeur. Look, for example, at Richard Decker's sweeping landscape on page 69, or Charles Saxon's monumental Venice on page 136. Or note the marvelously sodden atmosphere of Robert Weber's rainy city night on page 129, one of the wettest scenes imaginable; its atmosphere is utterly essential to the comedy.

As for dark airs of dread, of palpable, unspoken menace, no artist has done more in this particular vein than has Charles Addams. An example of how much Addams can derive from sheer suggestive atmosphere is his cartoon on page 70 of

---

* Originally appeared in *The New Yorker*, March 1, 1941.

the man reading off a long shopping list; the humor of the scene arises directly from that intangible but heavy mood which promises disaster all by itself.

In all of the above examples, too, there is displayed not only great technical skill in atmospheric scene painting, but a special deftness, or lack of ponderousness, characteristic of cartooning. The cartoonist's touch cannot be merely academic. He must paint his scene, however grandiose, but still be easy about it. His sense of selectivity, therefore, becomes another vital element; an expression in itself. As in all art, what the cartoonist chooses to leave out conveys as much as what he chooses to put in. Less is more.

And there are other elements, less obviously requisite to story telling. There is calligraphy, which perhaps expresses the *élan* and bounce of the cartoonist himself more than of his narrative. Mainly, it is a direct aesthetic joy. Another is texture; the smack of watercolor on rough paper, the cozy nubbliness of chalks, the forthright stroke of gouache impasto or the velvet sensuosity of charcoal. These elements enhance the purely visual enjoyment we derive from many a cartoon. Some specimens of outstanding calligraphy can be seen on pages 122, 124, 209, 211, and 212; and there is a deliciousness of texture to be found consistently in the work of such artists as Whitney Darrow, Jr., Edward Sorel, Barbara Shermund, Lee Lorenz and Eldon Dedini, to name just a few.

Then there is the pleasure we get from recognition of the artist's individuality, his personal style. Speak the names of Peter Arno, James Thurber, Charles Dana Gibson or Art Young. Each conjures up not just a drawing or two, but a *way* of drawing; a consistency of touch and observation, often of subject matter or theme, which runs through an entire body of work and reflects one personality.

Finally, there is that sense of conversation mind-to-mind, of the artist speaking through his work directly to the viewer. Few branches of the visual arts provide such opportunities for comment and opinion as does cartooning. Comment is *proper* to cartooning, whereas in many other art forms it is all-too-often forced. Both in his ideas and drawings—his observations of people, life styles, trends; even in the little visual asides of hands, feet, hair-do's—the cartoonist makes his personal response to the entirety of what he sees in the world around him. In fact, the only brake on the cartoonist's freest and most profound discourse is applied by editors; and a severe brake it is. Of course, every form of art has its complaining patrons and artists often can find ways of getting around them. In general, where the cartoonist is most nearly a free agent he observes and comments best. Where he is the long-term client of some one controlling periodical or syndicate his discourse is least interesting. Or at any rate, least varied.

It has not been the intention of this preface to discuss all aspects of cartooning. We do not, for instance, speak of the relationship of the cartoonist to his times. Nor do we even attempt to analyze his humor. Too much has been said by many an art historian or critic, writing in a forum such as this, about "the influence of new industrial technology on comic drawing," or "the humorist's peculiar worm's eye view of life." By contrast, surprisingly little has been offered on the very point these writers might be presumed most qualified to discuss, namely the art itself. We, therefore, have confined ourselves to that aspect alone; it is sufficient—and neglected—ground enough to try to cover in these few pages.

But let us touch on one more point. As noted, the cartoonist makes use of the whole range of those resources which together constitute the classic elements of art, such as composition, texture, selectivity, etc., and he uses them as fully and as purposefully as anyone in art today. But he enjoys another valuable resource—in fact, a priceless one in the contemporary art world.

The cartoonist is the beneficiary of an immediate, self-correcting "feedback" from his audience. He shows his work; the viewers laugh. Or they do not laugh. They do not feel intimidated, they never shrug evasively and murmur, "interesting." He knows at once if he succeeds or fails; and he can learn in both cases. He is enabled to grow in his work throughout the span of his career, guided by that unfailing touchstone—laughter. He cannot blunder very far along some solipsistic bypath without shortly being made aware of it. Nor can his drawings be mysteriously "puffed" by dealers to a docile public. The cartoonist's public enjoys, participates in and personally evaluates his art; it is a public which, therefore, will never stand to be deceived about him nor permit him to deceive himself.

All this is not to depict cartooning, necessarily, as the hidden El Dorado of the art world. Every cartoonist digging in this ground, however rich it may be, does not produce treasures. But it is time some serious attention was paid to those who do. There happen to be quite a number of them.

Many are presented in this book. The value of what they have mined cannot, of course, be proved in essays; it is a judgment best left to the eye of the beholder. Look and see. But notice, as you do, how much art there truly is in the art of cartooning.

EDWIN FISHER
MORT GERBERG

THE ART IN CARTOONING

THE
EARLY YEARS

1890s–1920s

REA IRVIN

CLUBS WE DO NOT CARE TO JOIN
The Darwin Club

THOMAS NAST

TWO STRIKES AND THE BASES FULL

FANNED OUT

CHARLES DANA GIBSON

18

THE RACE QUESTION—PRIVATELY AND PUBLICLY EXPLAINED

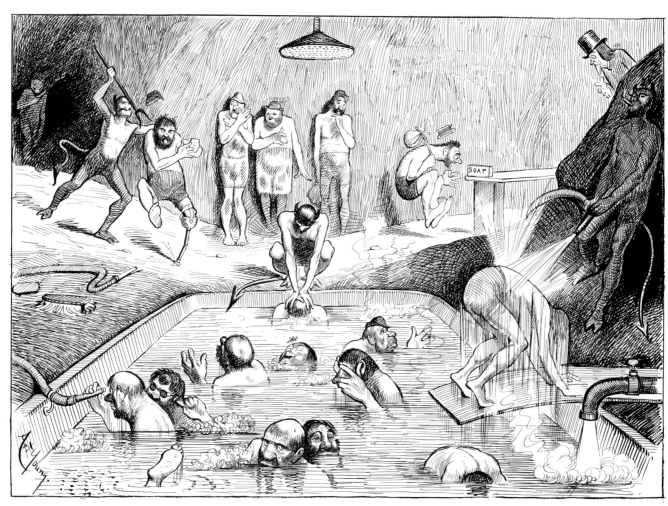

INFERNO

THOMAS NAST

FATHER REDUCES HIS WEIGHT

1

2

3

4

5

6

7

8

9

10

A. B. FROST

A. B. FROST

He made some hootch and tried it on the dog.

A. B. FROST

"Dat's a remarkable fine chile, Mis' Peebles, what name have you giv her?"
"Dat chile is so kind and gentle in her ways dat I was 'bleeged to fin' a
name fo' her dat was sof' and smoove so I calls her Ambrosia."

A. B. FROST

He really dislikes pets. But the man in the adjoining studio sings, yes he sings!

T. S. SULLIVANT

METHUSELAH HAS A BIRTHDAY PARTY

JOHN HELD, JR.

COVER: *"Horse Sense," Life,* ca. 1920.

RALPH BARTON

RALPH BARTON

T. S. SULLIVANT

IN THIS MECHANICAL AGE

(Willie, out driving for the first time.) *"Oh! Uncle, look at his nostrils. His steam's escaping."*

"What's the celebration about M's
	Milligan?"
"Sure, me boy's comin' home today. He
	was sentenced to ten years in the
	penitentiary, but he got three years off
	for good conduct."
"Ah! I wish _I_ had a son like that."

BOARDMAN ROBINSON

PETER ARNO

ZIM

"Yeh, an' if y' ever 'and me any more of
	yer mouf, I'll—"
"Gor! Watch the omnibus, dearie! The
	way yer standin' it'll catch yuh as
	pretty a one as ever I see—Whoops!"

*"If you will allow me
to say so I think
that is damnably odd."*

W. MORGAN

"Do you use your husband's name?"
He discovered her to be the wife
of his favorite novelist.

W. MORGAN

JACK MARKOW

"Pardon me, officer, can you tell me where they moved Hudson Street?"

T. S. SULLIVANT

MR. HO. *"I lost my balance as the street car started today and
    sat right in a monkey's lap."*

MRS. HO. *"Oh! I hope you apologized."*

MR. HO. *"No; it was too late, but I'm going to send a wreath."*

*"Cud ah have jes' one peek,
boss? Ah've always un'erstood
dere wuz machinery in 'em."*

R. B. FULLER

GLUYAS WILLIAMS

AT THE LIFE INSURANCE AGENTS' BANQUET

THE THIRTIES

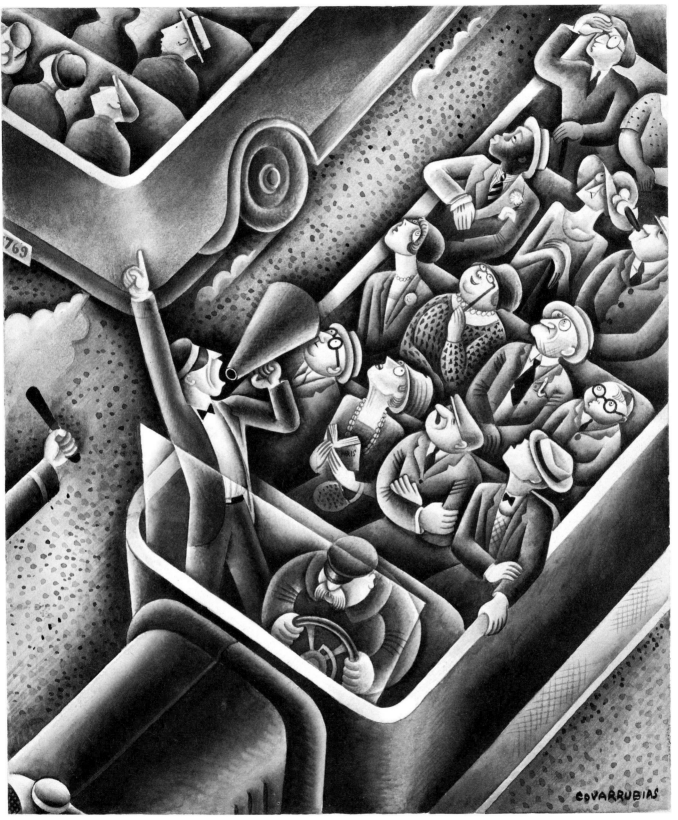

COVARRUBIAS

AL FRUEH

Man: *"Is Mr. Pinfield stopping here?"*

Clerk (formerly employed in a drug store): *"I'm sorry, Sir, we haven't got Mr. Pinfield, but we've got somebody just as good."*

O. SOGLOW

OTTO SOGLOW

THE BURGLER RETIRES

NATE COLLIER

"Oh, isn't it simply grand?"

BILL HOLMAN

THE STUDENT DENTIST PRACTICES AT HOME

CRAWFORD YOUNG

"Thank heaven this species will soon be extinct."

38

"Hello, New York Central Railroad? This is Rufus."

JACK KABAT

RUSSELL PATTERSON

FORBELL

LITTLE KNOWN OCCUPATIONS
Tuning Cuckoo Clocks

REA IRVIN

PREDICAMENT IN CONNECTICUT
Curious behavior of the Litchfield Hounds following their Broadway run
in "Uncle Tom's Cabin"

JAMES THURBER

"With you I've known peace, Lida, and now you say you're going crazy."

"If I knew this was such a swell joint, I'd 'a' dressed up a bit."

I. KLEIN

S. J. PERELMAN

I'M DOING PENNANTS FOR MY SHINS, BOYS, SNUFFLED THE REPENNANT SENIOR
The next flash will be Marcus Tullius Cicero boop-a-dooping his latest torch
number, *"Can't You Hear Me Calling, Catiline?"* *"What do you think of the
Amazon, Captain Bemis?"* sifted one of the pad-and-pencil boys. *"I was a fool
ever to have married her!"* gibbered the explorer. And for the deuce spot
Rafael Sabatini and Captain Blood will wow you with *"Singing in the Vein."*

"And how many carbons, Sir?"

JOHN HELD, JR.

LEARN TO DANCE "THE BIG APPLE" IN ONE EASY LESSON.

TROMBONE HITS VASE (A), SPILLING WATER ON SPONGE (B)-WEIGHT OF WATER IN SPONGE CAUSES STRING (C) TO OPEN BOX, RELEASING MOUSE (D)- CAT (E), SEEING MOUSE, RAISES BACK AND TILTS PLATFORM (F), SPILLING BIG APPLE ON PUPIL'S HEAD AND CAUSING HER TO GO SLIGHTLY GOOFY AND FALL INTO THE NATURAL MOVEMENTS OF "THE BIG APPLE".

RUBE GOLDBERG

C. D. RUSSELL

PETE

PERCY CROSBY

"Seems to me I oughta be able to do somethin' with this."

GILBERT BUNDY

"Where is Junior?"
"Now, George, I'm sure he didn't have a thing to do with this."

"It's the last time I ever help
a football team break training."

© 1939 The New Yorker Magazine, Inc.

BARBARA SHERMUND

ALICE HARVEY RAMSEY

"I'm so glad to be here and see Mother married. Both times before I was sick."

© 1930 The New Yorker Magazine, Inc.

"*Well, she's outdoorsy in a terracey sort of way.*"

GARDNER REA

RICHARD TAYLOR

"*She takes the place of the old free lunch.*"

RICHARD TAYLOR

"*Now, where the heck did that lion go?*"

JOHN GROTH

E. SIMMS CAMPBELL

"*And den I plugged him, semicolon----*"

LOUIS PRISCILLA

"John went out to buy some bullfrogs and crickets."

PERRY BARLOW

JOHN GROTH

"Me? I was a financial expert."

Congressman: *"I better give you the address of my fortune teller, Senator, she always gives me good advice on how to vote on difficult questions."*

I. KLEIN

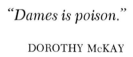

*"Would you say 'I hereby resign'—
or make it more informal, like 'I quit'?"*

DOROTHY McKAY

"Dames is poison."

DOROTHY McKAY

GLUYAS WILLIAMS

IMPRESSIONS OF MAGAZINE OFFICES—Good Housekeeping

56

DOROTHY McKAY

"One billion dollars on the red."

CARL ROSE

ED NOFZIGER

"My goodness, is that you? I thought all this was me!"

GLUYAS WILLIAMS

Headwaiters always take me for long walks in restaurants.

I. KLEIN

JACK MARKOW

"Wait 'til he sits down—there's a tack on his chair."

ED GRAHAM

GILBERT BUNDY

"You're right, Agnes—Faust's trousers are slipping."

"*A magnificent fowl, Madam. Notice how he looks you straight in the eye.*"

© 1938 The New Yorker Magazine, Inc.

GEORGE PRICE

HELEN HOKINSON

"*I shall now quote the passages I consider obscene.*"

© 1933 The New Yorker Magazine, Inc.

*"You can talk softly. Your mother
will think I'm making love to you."*

JOHN HELD, JR.

JAMES THURBER

THE WAR BETWEEN MEN AND WOMEN: VIII. "The Battle of Labrador"

RUSSELL PATTERSON

"My next apartment must have an elevator."

CARL ROSE

"All those in favor of Mr. Ford's offer for our village say 'Aye'!"

"In time the dog world will undoubtedly
have its Freuds and Jungs."

JAMES THURBER

"It's a sweetheart, gentlemen. The
nose contains a devastating
explosive and the middle section
a deadly gas. The tail is packed
with propaganda leaflets to be
read by the survivors."

© 1939 The New Yorker Magazine, Inc.

ROBERT DAY

66

OTTO SOGLOW

DOROTHY McKAY

"I told you she'd pack 'em in!"

WORLD WAR II
AND
POST WAR

RICHARD DECKER

"Wouldn't you love this in technicolor?"

CHARLES ADDAMS

"Now let's see—one sashweight, one butcher's cleaver, one galvanized iron tub, fifty feet of half-inch rope, one gunny sack, one electric torch, one pickaxe, one shovel, twenty pounds of quicklime, a box of cigars, and a beach chair."

"Of course, I'm paying attention! You said you were going to attempt
to pick up the handkerchief with your teeth."

PERRY BARLOW

"There! How do *you* like being
splashed?"

BARNEY TOBEY

"Are you unhappy, darling?"
"Oh, yes, yes! Completely."

© 1942 The New Yorker Magazine, Inc.

CHARLES ADDAMS

CHON DAY

"Hold it!"

SAM COBEAN

H. T. WEBSTER

The Timid Soul has read that gangsters occasionally carry machine guns in violin cases.

MOPEY DICK AND THE DUKE

D. WORTMAN

"What we don't know about gardening, Mopey, would just about fill a window box."

"Getting pretty fancy, isn't he?"

ED NOFZIGER

"...and they told us it's going to get worse."

ROBERT DAY

GREGORY d'ALESSIO

WELCOME HOME!—*"...and men, it's no picnic out there—you'll be entirely on your own! I know there isn't a coward among you ... so, synchronize your watches, and off you go at 21:30 ... Good luck, and drop me a line the minute you arrive in the States!"*

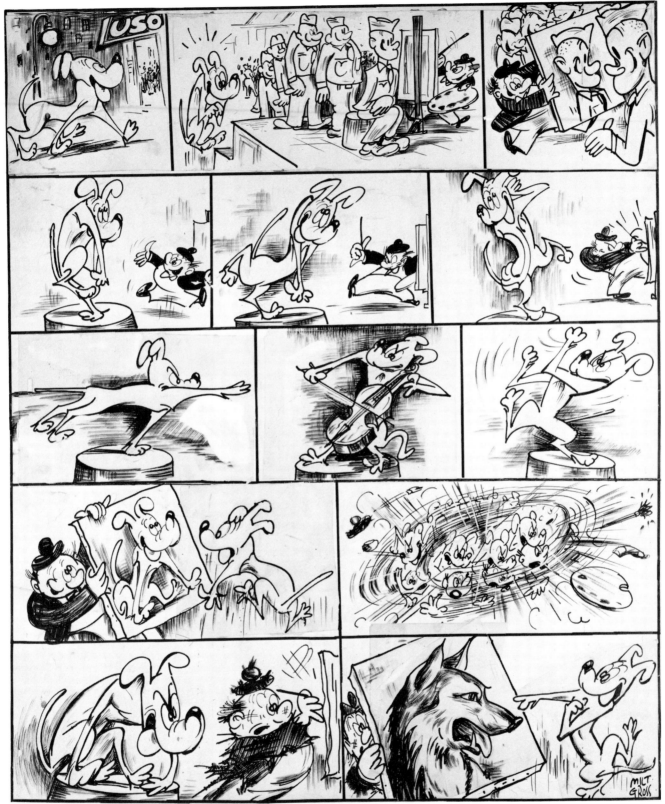

MILT GROSS

PETE

SYD HOFF

"*Phooey!*"

PETER ARNO

"Have you tried an oculist?"

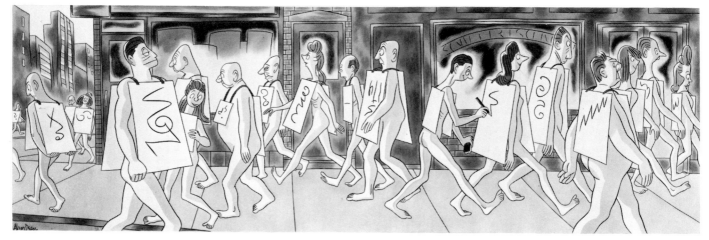

ABNER DEAN

Everyone must have a label

Amnesia Victim

ABNER DEAN

ABNER DEAN

ABNER DEAN

Very Bad Memory

ABNER DEAN

How much of me is me?

ABNER DEAN

The people at the next table are all idiots

"*Private Wilson reporting for duty.*"

JARO FABRY

LEO GAREL

"*Great Scott—I'm drafted.*"

PETER ARNO

"Which one? Great heavens, are you mad?"

84

CHARLES ADDAMS

"Don't feel bad, Nelson. With normal growth you'll be in there next year."

TOM HENDERSON

"Craig, show Joyce how you can stand on your head."

BORIS DRUCKER

*"Don't pay any attention to him,
he's 90% water."*

STAN AND JAN BERENSTAIN

COVER: *"Dancing School," Collier's*, March 4, 1950.

JOHN GALLAGHER

"One order 'Chef's Salad.'"

SAM COBEAN

ANATOL KOVARSKY

88

MARY PETTY

"A few years ago a contribution of a hundred thousand dollars would have been a cinch for Ambassadar to England. Now what do they offer me? Ambassador to Guatemala! How's that for inflation?"

GLENN BERNHARDT

"Cheer up, Gilbey, we're close to civilization!"

MARTIN GIUFFRE

". . . shovel, Jim Kenney; pick, Phil Pacony; sledgehammer, Ed Harkins---"

PERRY BARLOW

"Well, he says he can change a fifty-dollar bill. Now what?"

© 1944 The New Yorker Magazine, Inc.

"Well, all I can say is I hope nobody comes in here two thousand years from now and thinks we really looked like that."

© 1946 The New Yorker Magazine, Inc.

RICHARD DECKER

GARRETT PRICE

"If we can get some good jazz now it will be perfect."

H. T. WEBSTER

CIVILIZATION REACHES FULL FLOWER

VIRGIL PARTCH

PETS
BOUGHT
&
SOLD

PETS
BOUGHT
&
SOLD

O. SOGLOW

OTTO SOGLOW

94

VIRGIL PARTCH

"*Do we have any humble pie, this guy wants to know.*"

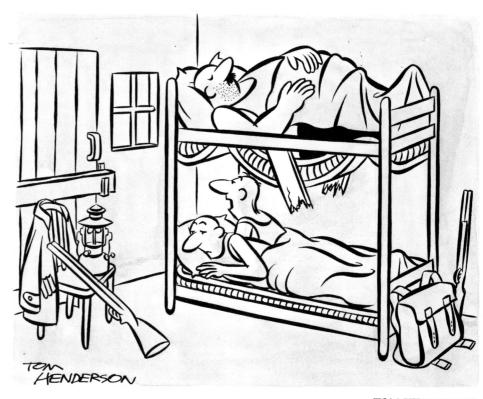

TOM HENDERSON

"*Something must be prowling around outside. I just heard a twig snap.*"

"... And this is the chaplain's office."

BIL KEANE

RICHARD TAYLOR

"Gad, Milton, can't you sing anything besides 'Seated One Day at the Organ'?"

PLATE 1

CONSTANTIN ALAJALOV

COVER: "The New Arrivals," *The Saturday Evening Post,* July 27, 1946.

PLATE 2

DOROTHY McKAY

*"I know the street is Broadway, dagnab it!! What I want to know is
the name of the town."*

PLATE 3

ELDON DEDINI

"Okay, lieutenant, so how would _you_ conduct this war if _you_ were president?"

PLATE 4

Ernest Hemingway as Tarzan.
COVARRUBIAS

HOWARD SHOEMAKER

PLATE 5

LEE LORENZ

"You've got to admit those people have natural rhythm."

PLATE 6

FISH

COVER: *Vanity Fair*, March, 1921.

PLATE 7

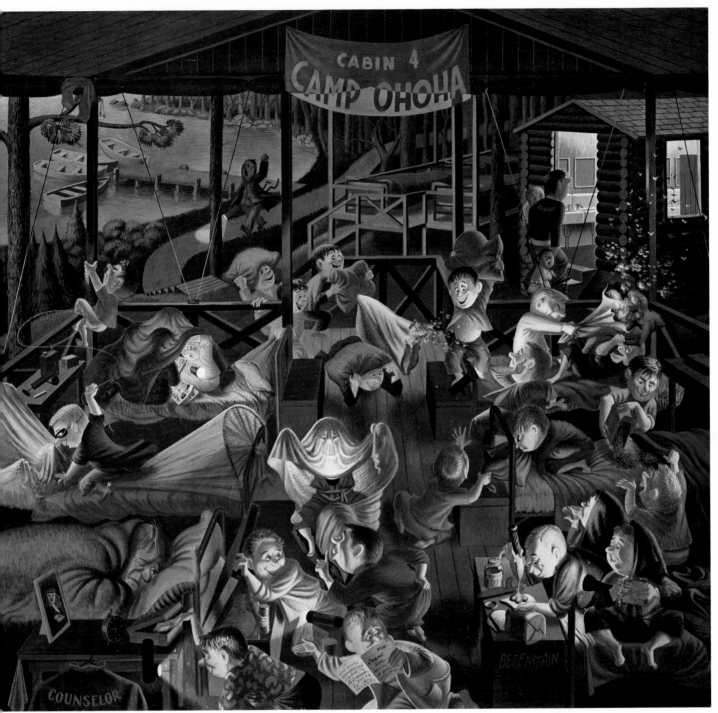

STAN AND JAN BERENSTAIN

COVER: "Summer Camp," *Collier's*, July 15, 1950.

PLATE 8

AL SWILLER

"Look, Toulouse, I paint what I see!"

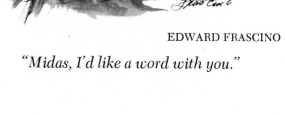

EDWARD FRASCINO

"Midas, I'd like a word with you."

"It's broken—I guess we'll have to talk."

MARTHA BLANCHARD

PLATE 9

"Thank you madam, but the pencils are not for sale."

AL SWILLER

PLATE 10

ROWLAND B. WILSON

"I don't mind it really—I'm only here to gather material for a book."

PLATE 11

Cardinal Cooke takes confession from Andy Warhol.

EDWARD SOREL

Ziegler, Ruckelshaus, Kleindienst, Shultz, Ehrlichman, Klein, Haldeman and Kissinger march in New York's Steuben Day parade.

EDWARD SOREL

PLATE 12

COVARRUBIAS

IMPOSSIBLE INTERVIEW—John D. Rockefeller Senior versus Josef Stalin.

OPPOSITE: COVER, *Punch*, July 4, 1973.

PLATE 13

ARNOLD ROTH

PLATE 14

HOWARD BAER

"I like you older men—young men are so broke."

JARO FAB

*"He's paying me fifty thousand dollars to get back his
letters but I'm retaining the movie rights."*

PLATE 15

RICHARD TAYLOR

"Harry has no interest in mundane pleasures."

PLATE 16

CHARLES SAXON

"The Closed Mind." Experimental drawing in watercolor and crayon.

NED HILTON

"Someday the public will demand more than a big vehicle with a lot of horse power."

JOHN GALLAGHER

"Sometimes I wish he'd never shot the darn thing!"

JOHN HELD, JR.

EDWIN LEPPER

*"Here's how it works. First you organize the kids. Then you threaten
to walk out unless you get an ice cream break every morning."*

99

CHON DAY

AL KAUFMAN

"Tell me—where else can you get a twelve-fold tie?"

B. WISEMAN

"This will set our work back fifty years."

GREGORY d'ALESSIO

"The liquor has run out, Sir!"

JOHN DEMPSEY

"It doesn't say swimming pool, does it?"

WHITNEY DARROW, JR.

"All right, Haskell—sell me."

"Not one word about Freedom Fighters in all of DAS KAPITAL."

DAVID PASCAL

ROBERT KRAUS

"I say the only good Indian is a dead Indian. Present company excepted, of course."

© 1957 The New Yorker Magazine, Inc.

PETER ARNO

"It feels like it might be a grain of sand."

ED FISHER

"Well, that settles it. There __was__ intelligent life on Mars!"

"But first, our national anthem."

ROBERT KRAUS

DANA FRADON

"Ouch, damn it!"

ED FISHER

"Rat! . . . Squealer! . . . Double-crosser!   *. . . Communist!"*

107

TED KEY

"Jeepers!"

NED HILTON

*"What is so new about a war on poverty?
I've been fighting one for years."*

"He said no, thanks, he'd rather stay with his own kind!"

DAVID LEVINE

ED NOFZIGER

"All Clear!"

DANA FRADON

"That'll be the day!"

© 1959 The New Yorker Magazine, Inc.

"You are charged with disorderly conduct, indecent exposure, and impersonating an officer."
© 1950 The New Yorker Magazine, Inc.

WHITNEY DARROW, JR.

GEORGE PRICE

"A simple 'yes' or 'no' will be sufficient, Madame."
© 1940 The New Yorker Magazine, Inc.

Mirachi

JOSEPH MIRACHI

"Well, you might have stopped it before it got this far."

WILLIAM von RIEGEN

"I suppose it's his wife who's spreading those nasty truths about me!"

WILLIAM von RIEGEN

"I'll give him credit for one thing; no matter how big you are, he'll still double-cross you."

SYD HOFF

"Mind if we freshen up a bit?"

BO BROWN

"To the ladies."

"Sam? Oh, the other night he jumped up, said, 'Man, it's good to be alive' and walked out. That's the last we've seen of him."

JOHN DEMPSEY

ELDON DEDINI

"Communism is when the leader goes on the wagon, the whole damn country goes on the wagon."

CHON DAY

"This looks like a good place."

BORIS DRUCKER

"Do you have something with a smaller check?"

SYD HOFF

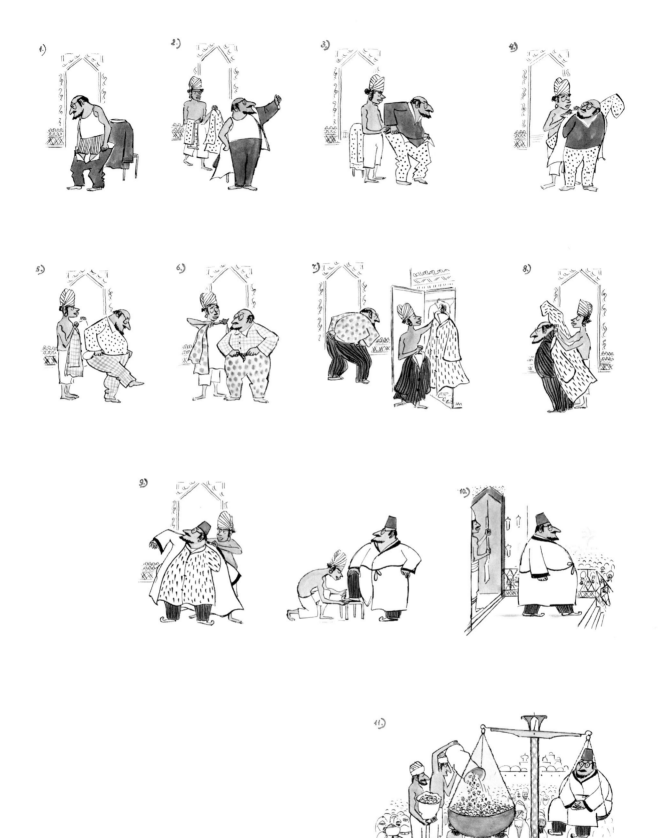

ANATOL KOVARSKY
© 1956 The New Yorker Magazine, Inc.

CARL ROSE

"I never could tell the difference between a stalactite
and a stalagmite."

JOHN GALLAGHER

"Why don't you hang out the window like other dogs?"

ELDON DEDINI

"Here's the stuff you wanted, comrade. I simply sent out questionnaires to thirty thousand people, coast to coast, and got a fantastic response."

118

WHITNEY DARROW, JR.

"The party's been called off. Helen has the virus."

SYVERSON

HENRY SYVERSON

CHARLES ADDAMS

"... and if it's a boy we're going to give it a Biblical name like Cain or Ananias."

THE
CURRENT
PERIOD

1960–1975

ROWLAND B. WILSON

"When shall we open fire, Sir?"

DONALD REILLY

"Let us rap."

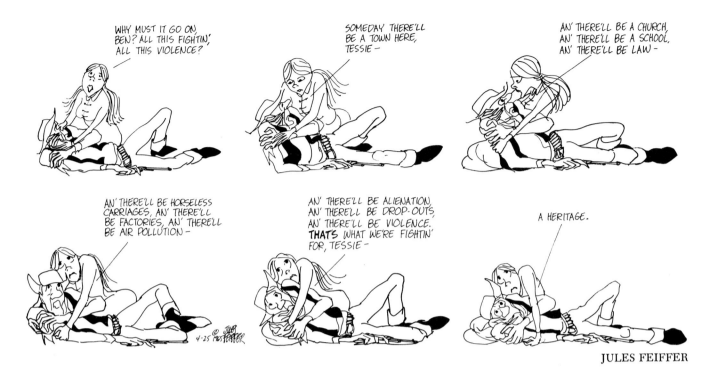

JULES FEIFFER

SERGIO ARAGONES

"Aha! Voice of America!"

© 1962 The New Yorker Magazine, Inc.

DINK SIEGEL

*"Resisting arrest and
impersonating an officer."*

© 1962 The New Yorker Magazine, Inc.

FRANK MODELL

PETER ARNO

"It's an oink oink here, an oink oink there— here an oink, there an oink, everywhere an oink oink!"

JOSEPH MIRACHI

"He's fast and clever and he's got a wallop that really hurts. In fact, in my opinion, he's one of the greatest!"

ORLANDO BUSINO

"You're going home to WHAT mother?"

JARED LEE

J. B. HANDELSMAN

"Of course war brutalizes people. What doesn't?"

128

LEE LORENZ

R. O. BLECHMAN

ROBERT WEBER

"Playboy."

WILLIAM O'BRIAN

"Grand Central and step on it!"

"Can your little girl come out and play?"

BETTY SWORDS

BARNEY TOBEY

"Mother!"

ALAN DUNN

"It's sheer, unadulterated sex, and we're all for it. Now to make our lawyers happy,
would it cramp your style to work in a little material of redeeming social importance?"

© 1966 The New Yorker Magazine, Inc.

"I suppose it's fitting that we should
stand. After all, we'll outlive them."

ABE CRAMER

CHARLES RODRIGUES

"Hey, man, would you hold my sign while I go for a sandwich?"

134

ROWLAND B. WILSON

GEORGE BOOTH

"Your bill came to forty-eight dollars more than we estimated, because that little black thing with a lot of wires going into it needed fixing."

ROLAND MICHAUD

"Oops, sorry."

CHARLES SAXON

"Marcelline, there's something I must tell you. I'm only here on a 14-to-21 day excursion plan."

AL ROSS

"It's true you've made me happy, but, did making me happy, make <u>you</u> happy?"

C. E. M.

"I wonder, Sir, if I could have your daughter's head—er—hand in marriage?"

ED FISHER

*"It just shows what colossal achievements man is capable of when he stops spending
all his time, energy and resources on war."*

"...weather permitting, of course."

WILLIAM HOEST

Lost and Found

PHIL INTERLANDI

"It was a brown paper bag and inside was
a fifth of—Oh, forget it."

"Now, let's take a look at where it's going."

JAMES MULLIGAN

JAMES STEVENSON

"This the way to the turnpike? We're escaping from a Senior Citizens' Planned Community."

© 1962 The New Yorker Magazine, Inc.

PHIL INTERLANDI

"*Are you sure we have the right address, Martha?*"

LEE LORENZ

"... and, of course, the Bell Telephone Labs and R.C.A. In addition, may we extend our thanks
to the following sub-contractors who helped to make this expedition successful ..."

"I'll stop calling you 'Maw' if
you stop calling me 'Paw'."

DEAN VIETOR

SIDNEY HARRIS

"No, that was McNamara. Dean Rusk ordered ham on rye."

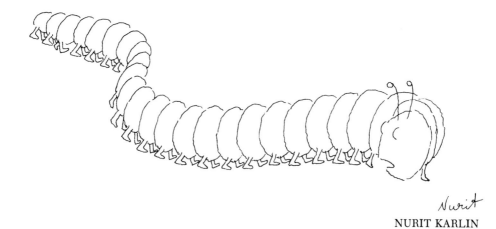

NURIT KARLIN

"Twenty-two is out of step. Pass it on."

EVERETT OPIE

"Now just between you and me and the lampost."

ARNOLDO FRANCHIONI

"It's nothing personal, Prescott. It's just that a higher court gets a kick out of overruling a lower court."

SIDNEY HARRIS

"You been givin' any thought to what you're gonna do after you drop out?"

MORT GERBERG

"*Are you an emergency?*"

DEAN VIETOR

JULES FEIFFER

148

CLAUDE SMITH

CHARLES BARSOTTI

"Through no fault of my own, Sir, I was drawn very small and with the left hand."

149

ED FISHER

"The young people don't seem to believe in anything these days!"

JOHN RUGE

"... And, while each subsidiary company will have a certain amount of fiscal autonomy, all major policy decisions will rest with the parent corporation and its board of directors. However ..."

"What did we ever do with our evenings, Henry, before we became <u>*aware?*</u>*"*

JAMES WEAVER

DICK OLDDEN

"This is a recording—but the person who made the recording is a warm, compassionate human being."

MARVIN TANNENBERG

AL JOHNS

PETER PORGES

ED ARNO

"So they moved to the suburbs, swapped wives, and lived happily ever after."

JACK ZIEGLER

Kliban

B. KLIBAN

"Hi, there, big fellah! I'm Spike Merton of Batner, Bitten and Burton—how would you like to try a man's cigarette?"

BILL MURPHY

BOB BRANDRETH

GEORGE BOOTH

"Your seeming indifference to the matter of your past-due account is difficult to understand. We have every confidence in you and believe that you intend to pay, but your account has now reached the stage where we can no longer simply continue making requests for payment . . ."

"*I'll tell you where the action is.*
First you get a haircut, <u>then</u> you get your allowance."

CHARLES SAXON

W. MILLER

BILL LEE

"Somehow I don't trust this new apostle."

"I gave at the office."

BRUCE COCHRAN

*"What's the point of hiring a Negro
if he doesn't look like a Negro?"*

LEE LORENZ

160

DON OREHEK

"It's her last wish upon retiring after twenty-five years!"

"It's your Godmother."

BERNARD SCHOENBAUM

J. B. HANDELSMAN

"I was packaged by Candidates Limited. Who packaged you?"

TODAY each copy of
BEST SHORT STORIES
will be autographed by
ALL the AUTHORS

GEORGE PRICE

JAMES STEVENSON
© 1964 The New Yorker Magazine, Inc.

VAHAN SHIRVANIAN

S. GROSS

"*Don't be alarmed. We're an encounter group.*"

MAL HANCOCK

"*He says slithering is passe.*"

JOHN RUGE

"I always maintain that anything written on <u>two</u> sides of a mountain
could be said just as well on <u>one</u> side of a mountain!"

DONALD REILLY

HOWARD SHOEMAKER

"For God's sake, Miss Wilson,
don't bother with Philip Roth!
Save Galsworthy!"

HENRY MARTIN

BRIAN SAVAGE

*"It took me three years to smuggle this out, and it's been rejected
by every publishing house in the West."*

STAN HUNT

"Did you ever notice how like attracts like?"

EVERETT OPIE

"No more for me, Joe."

CHARLES SAXON

"Did someone in here buzz?"

1

2

3

4

5

6

CLAUDE SMITH

LOU MYERS

MISCHA RICHTER

"Well, I can see that nothing has changed for the women."

GEORGE BOOTH

"One of the choir boys tells me Ralph Nader is hiding in the lilies."

"*They're leaving to be recycled.*"

© 1971 The New Yorker Magazine, Inc.

EDWARD KOREN

KOREN

THE SENSUOUS HIPPO

JOHN CALDWELL

VAHAN SHIRVANIAN

"One of these days, baby, one of these days . . ."

ORLANDO BUSINO

"Run for your life! It's boredom, spawned by technological advances and overabundance of leisure."

MISCHA RICHTER

"Wow! You mean they got all this in exchange for just one Van Gogh?"

"*It all began when I decided to get involved in the events of our time.*"

JOSEPH FARRIS

S. GROSS

WILLIAM HAMILTON

"I'm crazy about your image, Ray, who made it?"

RICHARD McCALLISTER

"So often I find myself at a loss for words. What do you say when people hold you to their ears?"

CHARLES BARSOTTI

"First thing you know we'll need a filing cabinet."

BARNEY TOBEY

"No, I've never been to Paris. In fact, I've never been out of the States."

HERB BRAMMEIER, JR.

*"Then it's agreed—one million for research in recycling
and two million to publicize it."*

ROBERT CENSONI

"The freezer broke."

MAL HANCOCK

"I go 'bump' in the night. What do you do?"

"He's furious! We hung his painting upside down."

JOSEPH FARRIS

"Your son needn't be a student. As a dropout, he is eligible for our special Young Punk fares."

J. B. HANDELSMAN

"I appreciate your asking me to join the Klan, man, but I think you got a wrong number."

MARVIN TANNENBERG

ED ARNO

"You only bring peace; I bring income-tax exemption!"

WOODMAN

BILL WOODMAN

"Hot dogs, hamburgers, and french fries!"

KOREN

EDWARD KOREN

"The sex isn't too good, but the violence is marvelous."

LOU MYERS

DIANE DENEROFF

"I think my wife is fooling around with the plumber!"

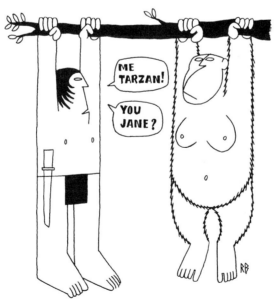

BOB BRANDRETH

GEORGE DOLE

"Hey, Joe! It's the hospital—your wife just had 3 of a kind."

ROBERT WEBER

"Give us a kiss."

MARVIN TANNENBERG

"Writing another one of your little protest songs, Mr. Key—?"

GET WELL CARDS

"If you think it's so amusing <u>you</u> send it, but I'm not signing <u>my</u> name to it."

STAN HUNT

AL ROSS

"To hell with rising prices, I say. Let's live!"

CHILDREN'S GAMES OF THE SEVENTIES

Charlie Manson Says

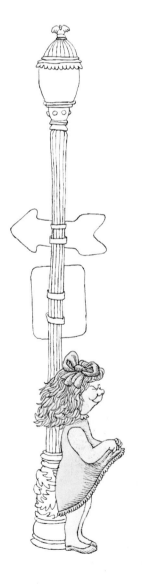

Hide and Go Seek

Red Light

Vietnam

Electrocute the Drunk

GAHAN WILSON

WILLIAM O'BRIAN

*"We've had a lot of fun fixing up this place, but you know how it is—
whenever you think you're done, there's always something else to do."*

PETER PORGES

HERB BRAMMEIER, JR.

HENRY SYVERSON

AL KAUFMAN

"He can't be much of a doctor. He's never written
a book on diet or sex."

DICK OLDDEN

MORT GERBERG

"Are you _sure_ this is fire?"

"Does everyone take sugar?"

C. E. M.

HERBERT GOLDBERG

"Maynard, your private face is showing."

"... and do you, Kim, vow to strip beds, and do you, John, vow to remake beds until death do you part?"

MARY GAUERKE

BOB MERZ

DONALD REILLY

"What's the best way to send laundry to Canada?"

WILLIAM HOEST

*"I expect one hundred per cent perfection around here, Perkins,
or Walters, or whatever your name is."*

M. K. BROWN

DON OREHEK

"You were right, Dad, that mini-skirt was too short."

MIKE WITTE

*"It's too good to be true, Edna—my son the doctor a partner
with your son the malpractice lawyer . . ."*

MAL HANCOCK

BERNARD SCHOENBAUM

*"Urology Department.
Can you hold?"*

LARRY KATZMAN

JACK ZIEGLER

MISCHA RICHTER

"Nice weaseling on the pill!"

HENRY MARTIN

"Hail, hail the gang's all here! What the heck do
we care? What the heck do we care . . ."

ROLAND MICHAUD

"I think I'll drop out and get drafted. It's safer than going to college."

HENRY SYVERSON

"*I take it you believe in God.*"
BILL MURPHY

ED FRASCINO

"*Remember that Christmas you sold your watch to buy me a comb and
I sold my hair to buy you a watch fob?*"

ALDEN ERIKSON

JAMES STEVENSON

"Oh, nothing much—just reading the Sunday 'Times.' What are you doing?"

PETER PORGES

"That's my dauphin!"

MORT GERBERG

"Listen, man, just because I don't _act_ hostile doesn't mean I don't _feel_ hostile."

216

"It's hard to believe that
someday we'll be just so much nostalgia."

WILLIAM HAMILTON

". . . and that's <u>Ms</u>. Muffet to you!"

MARY GAUERKE

ROBERT WEBER

"Where's the forest? All I can see is the trees."

MORT GERBERG

". . . When do I want my vacation? Uh, how about the first two hours in August?"

ROBERT CENSONI

"Did it ever occur to you that with all the eggs we've laid there should be more of us?"

"That's the difference between a recession and a depression."

BRIAN SAVAGE

WOODMAN

BILL WOODMAN

HERBERT GOLDBERG

"Pay no attention to me—I'm just a Gibbon chronicling our times."

CHARLES RODRIGUES

HERBERT GOLDBERG

"We'll have a boy and a girl, and then call it a day."

INDEX OF ARTISTS